Illumen
Summer 2024

Edited by
Tyree Campbell

Illumen
Summer 2024

Edited by Tyree Campbell

Cover art "Upon Reflection" by Paula Hammond
Cover design by Laura Givens

Vol. XXI, No. 4   June 2024

Illumen [ISSN: 1558-9714] is published quarterly on the 1st days of January, April, July, and October in the United States of America by Hiraeth Publishing, P.O. Box 1248, Tularosa, NM 88352. Copyright 2024 by Hiraeth Publishing. All rights revert to authors and artists upon publication except as noted in selected individual contracts. Nothing may be reproduced in whole or in part without written permission from the authors and artists. Any similarity between places and persons mentioned in the fiction or semi-fiction and real places or persons living or dead is coincidental. Writers and artists guidelines are available online at www.albanlake.com/guidelines. Guidelines are also available upon request from Hiraeth Publishing, P.O. Box 1248, Tularosa, NM 88352, if request is accompanied by a SASE #10 envelope with a 60-cent US stamp. Editor: Tyree Campbell. Subscriptions: $28 for one year [4 issues], $54 for two years [8 issues]. Single copies $10.00 postage paid in the United States. Subscriptions to Canada: $32 for one year, $54 for two years. Single copies $12.00 postage paid to Canada. U.S. and Canadian subscribers remit in U.S. funds. All other countries inquire about rates.

New from Terrie Leigh Relf!!
Postcards From Space

Terrie Leigh Relf loves sending and receiving postcards from the four corners of the universe—and beyond! Postcards tell a story. They are mementos from friends and family—and from total strangers—and provide a glimpse into life's journeys, observations, and adventures.

Here are some messages on postcards from space, found aboard a derelict craft that crashed on an arid, lifeless world. The OSPS (Outer Space Postal Service) has delivered these messages to Terrie, who now presents them to you. This is what it is like out there.

https://www.hiraethsffh.com/product-page/postcards-from-space-by-terrie-leigh-relf

A Little Help, Please

In the world of the small indie press we fight a never-ending battle for attention to our work, as writers and in publishing. Here's an example: big publishers [you know who they are] have gobs of $$$ that they can devote to advertising and marketing. Here at Hiraeth Publishing, our advertising budget consists of the deposits for whatever soda bottles and aluminum cans we can find alongside the highways. Anti-littering laws make our task even more difficult . . . ☺

That's where YOU come in. YOU are our best promoter. YOU are the one who can tell others about us. Just send 'em to our website, tell them about our store. That's all. Just that.

Of course, we don't mind if you talk us up. We're pretty good, you know. We have some award-winning and award-nominated writers and artists, plus other voices well-deserving to be heard [not everyone wins awards, right?] but our publications are read-worthy nevertheless.

That number once again is:

www.hiraethsffh.com

Friend us on Facebook at Hiraeth Publish and follow us on Twitter at

@HiraethPublish1

Contents

Features

- 13   The Inspiration for Galérien by Deborah Sheldon
- 24-32   Featured Poet: Lee Clark Zumpe
- 37   The Guy Belleranti Page
- 41-44   Featured Poet: Allister Nelson

Poems

- 8   Lumbee Legend by William Landis
- 12   Galérian by Deborah Sheldon
- 15   Thoughts Rising by Amanda Niamh Dawson
- 16   Poe Grows Old by Tyree Campbell
- 19   What Has This Modern Prometheus Done to My Body by Francis W. Alexander
- 20   Weathered Stone by Nick Ozment
- 21   Not the Candles by Devan Barlow
- 36   Forbidden Haibun: K2-18B by Francis W. Alexander
- 37   Ku by K. S. Hardy
- 38   Cinderella's Coachmen by K. S. Hardy
- 39   They Rattle Past in the Dark by Holly Day
- 40   The Beauty of a Changeling by Kellee Kranendonk
- 45   Defect by Debby Feo
- 46   Not Cupid's Arrows by Shawn Vimislicky
- 47   A Goldilocks Alien Exploration of the Solar System by Francis W. Alexander
- 48   Nuit's Garden by Anthony Bernstein
- 49   The Heart of the Song by Holly Day
      Lifeboats by Amanda Niamh Dawson
- 50   The Old Fisherman by Joy Yin

Illustrations

18   Mournful Specter by Sandy DeLuca
33   Belladonna by Sandy DeLuca

SUBSCRIBE TO ILLUMEN!!

We'll be glad you did…
So will you.
Here's the link:

https://www.hiraethsffh.com/product-page/illumen-1

Support the small independent press!

You're not afraid of a little poetry, are you?

The Miseducation of the Androids
By William Landis

What happens when androids confront concepts inconsistent with their programming? William Landis examines this question by means of flash fiction and haiku that you will find pithy, poignant, and amusing.

William Landis is a science fiction poet from North Carolina. He is a graduate of North Carolina A&T State University, completing both undergraduate, and graduate work in agriculture. He is currently working on a vermicomposting project, and he is an Army reserve engineer officer. He enjoys running, writing, reading, and exploring new places.

Order a copy here: https://www.hiraethsffh.com/product-page/miseducation-of-the-androids-by-william-landis

Lumbee Legend
William Landis

We stood together in the swamp,
Growing together like two cypress trees.
I wrapped my branches around her trunk.

Crickets hummed and frogs sang,
Fireflies twinkled like stars.
Suddenly,
A plop in the water behind us.

I told her the Lumbee Indian legend,
The story of swamp demons,
The tale only the old folks knew,

How a Confederate army had once marched in
And, except for screams and gunfire,
They were never heard from again.

Through black willow hair
She smiled up at me and said,
"I remember. I was there."

Midnight Comes Early
By Marcie Lynn Tentchoff

Marcie Lynn Tentchoff lives on the west coast of Canada, in a forest of brambles and evergreens far too densely tangled to form the setting for any but the darkest of fairy tales. She writes poetry and stories that tiptoe worriedly along the border of speculation and horror, and is an active member of both the Science Fiction & Fantasy Poetry Association and the Horror Writers Association. Marcie is an Aurora Award winner, and her work has been either nominated, short, or long-listed for Stoker, Rhysling, and British Fantasy awards. She is very much involved in middle grade and YA media, and edits Spaceports & Spidersilk, a magazine aimed at readers from 8-9 up to (and past!) 89. When she is not involved with the practice of placing and editing words on a page, she teaches creative writing and acting for a performing arts studio.

Order a copy here...

https://www.hiraethsffh.com/product-page/midnight-comes-early-by-marcie-lynn-tentchoff

Galérien
Deborah Sheldon

They lash our backs, and boom the drum.
The timbers of our galley thrum
as missiles hit – will we succumb?

I haul my oar, sweat grimed, mind dull;
the other ship, propelled by scull
advances, rams, destroys our hull.

Our broken boards let in the sea.
We list and flood, brine covers me;
my shackles bite, I can't get free.

This ship of slaves is sinking down,
a dance of corpses all around.
And yet, I find I cannot drown?

Our ship hits bottom, splits its keel,
the fishes flock in frenzied zeal.
We oarsmen will become their meal.

Is every man the same as me?
Their bodies dead, subsumed by sea
but minds alive to some degree?

Upon the sandy ocean floor
the shrimps, and crabs, and beasts galore
start feasting on our wretched store.

They nibble at my hands and feet –
soon, leg consumed of all its meat
releases me from iron cleat.

I float towards the ocean's skin,
a blighted soul, a demon, djinn,
when shark bite tears my abdomen.

Gases leave my belly fast,
I start to sink again, aghast,
back down to mandibles I'm cast.

Now on the ocean floor I lay
as creatures gnaw my brains away.
When nothing's left, I'll die…I pray.

The Inspiration for Galérien
Deborah Sheldon

I write fiction across the darker spectrum of horror and noir, and only came to poetry quite recently; my first poem was published in 2020. Throughout 2022 I studied poetry, aiming to pen my own attempts across a range of historical forms. At the time of writing, various magazines (including *Illumen*) have published 12 of my poems – one of which is shortlisted for an Australian Shadows Award. Definitely a strong incentive to keep going!

What I enjoy most about writing poetry in traditional forms is the discipline of rhyme and meter. It's not easy to construct a story that adheres to a rhyming scheme, yet doesn't feel overly contrived in its delivery. When writing, I keep a rhyming dictionary open and at the ready. Nevertheless, many more lines get jettisoned than kept, in my experience.

My poem "Galérien" is a triplet, which is a rare poetic choice these days. In fact, editor Tyree Campbell informs me that "Galérien" is the first triplet ever published in *Illumen* magazine. How wonderful to break new ground!

The triplet is a play on the tercet, which is a poem with three-line stanzas. What distinguishes the triplet from the tercet is that all three lines must share the same end sound. (Tercets permit different end sounds.) The triplet's rhyming pattern is AAA, BBB, CCC, DDD, and so on. This pattern is also known as a mono-rhyme. Historians believe that the triplet first made its appearance in the mid-sixteenth century, and came about when English writers desired a variation on the couplet.

To add to the trickiness, every line in a triplet must have the same number of syllables. I chose eight, simply because it's a common number in other poetic forms I've used, such as the décima espinela.

"Galérien" was inspired by my flash-fiction story, "Cast Down". The ship of a galley slave, chained to his oar, is in mid-battle when the hull is breached. Through "Galérien", I wanted to explore loss of autonomy over one's body. My first-person POV narrator is firstly a captive before transforming into something that is also, disturbingly, outside his control.

Thoughts Rising
Amanda Niamh Dawson

Minds ache to be free
But all are lost at sea
Scriptures to hold
Tongues too bold
Hold up your light
Behold seventh sight
Of matter sworn
Of ideals born
Virtues torn
Grace worn
Down by fears
Of life left longing
To fill some years

The trees will beckon
Step inside them
Air will lend them
Beams to guide them
All across the sphere
To the here
Already near

Poe Grows Old
Tyree Campbell

Hear the bottles with the pills—
    Tablet pills!
What a world of healthfulness their clattering distills!
      How they rattle, rattle, rattle,
      In the morning, noon, and night!
    While the vitamins that clinkle
    And metoprolol does sprinkle
      To the very heart's delight;
    With each beat, beat, beat,
    In a pillbox sort of treat,
To the polypillilation that so healthfully spills
    From the pills, pills, pills, pills,
      Pills, pills, pills—
From the rattling in the bottles of the pills.

The newest from G. O. Clark!!!

Mindscapes

G. O. Clark takes on the future in this riveting collection of poetic observations about life, the Universe, and everything else. He takes you up mountains and down valleys, and always makes you wonder about what's happening and what will happen (if we aren't careful).

Ordering links:
Print: https://www.hiraethsffh.com/product-page/mindscapes-by-g-o-clark
ePub: https://www.hiraethsffh.com/product-page/mindscapes-by-g-o-clark-2
PDF: https://www.hiraethsffh.com/product-page/mindscapes-by-g-o-clark-1

Mournful Specter by Sandy DeLuca

What Has This Modern Prometheus Done to My Body?
Francis W. Alexander

A mighty, but divided nation am I.
Once, I sailed the seven seas.
Now, I have the schizophrenic feel
of diverse oceans.
After I was awakened from eternal sleep,
these limbs were like barnacles on skin
slowly forming symbiotic relationships.

Now, they are a hinderance
when I try to eat, walk, or run.
When angry, my tongue curls zombie talk
instead of cursing like a sailor.
The people call me "his monster".
They don't comprehend a fish
attempting to swim faster to escape
when it is placed in a different medium
from that it is accustomed to.
They don't know that despite
what my countenance and limbs might dictate,
I still need wine, women, and song.

Weathered Stone
Nick Ozment

A pair of young lovers
Might walk across the moldering ground
And see a weathered stone
That is almost falling down,
And one of them will say
"I wonder who that was."

And if you could but speak
You would say,
"It was me.
Someday it will be you
But it was me.

"Breathe every breath child.
Savor holding your lover's hand,
Because you'll be under
Ground far longer than
You'll be above land.

"How very strange it will be
When all around you are graves
And on every stone is
An old familiar name."

Not the Candles
Devan Barlow

Just once, I would like to light a candle
Pleasant pine, or lavender
Anything to dull the smell of neighbors smoking
And not see, atop the wick
Other people within the flame

They are flames from the past,
Or another dimension (I've got no idea)
Groups of adventuring companions
Or lone, rugged souls
Fearing wolf-howls and enemy hoofbeats

They've always got treasure,
Tasks from some wizard, scars from dreadful dungeons
And they are always convinced
The mysterious face in the flame
Has something oracular to tell them

I've tried a dozen brands
It's not the candles, it's me
The place is full of discarded candles
And I want my apartment to smell nice
Without having to dispense destiny

Pittsburgh
and Other Poems
By Alan Ira Gordon

Pittsburgh and Other Poems

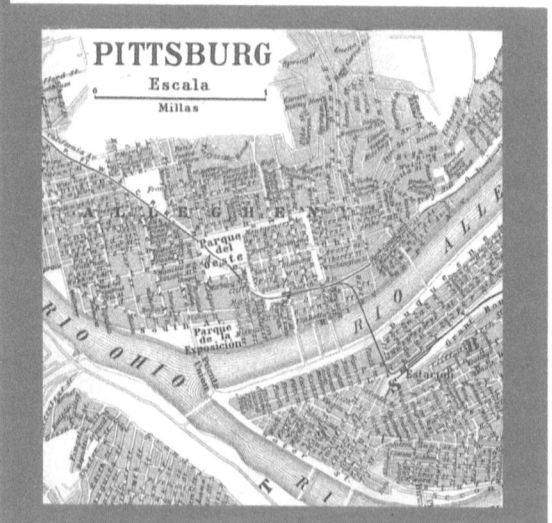

Alan Ira Gordon

Sometimes a sense of place is easy to identify and understand. In those instances, it can be a physical city, town, neighborhood or just a piece of property. Other times it can be a point in time, either past, present or future. And in yet other instances it can be a more exotic or alien sense of place, perhaps intergalactic, or multi-universe, even an alternate reality version of a well-known place and time, existing at a quantum point or merely within the minds of writers and readers.

All of the poems in this book explore in poetic form various ideas of sense of place, whether physical locations, points in time or ideas of place that could only exist (for now, at least) within the creative realms of science fiction, fantasy and/or horror.

Ordering links:
Print: https://www.hiraethsffh.com/product-page/pittsburgh-other-poems-by-alan-ira-gordon
ePub: https://www.hiraethsffh.com/product-page/pittsburgh-other-poems-by-alan-ira-gordon-2
PDF: https://www.hiraethsffh.com/product-page/pittsburgh-other-poems-by-alan-ira-gordon-1

FEATURED POET:
Lee Clark Zumpe

a dark and ancient souterrain

I saw them one misty morning,
in one of the sprawling valleys
beneath the shadow of the Mourne Mountains –

in a lush green meadowland,
enfolded by an impenetrable forest wall,
outside a dark and ancient souterrain,

its entrance overgrown with biting stonecrop,
a thicket of thorn-bushes mustered
to safeguard their secret passage.

I saw them one Midsomer night,
fairy-lights ablaze beneath the star-filled heavens,
dancing in the fitful moonlight –

far removed from Oberon's stern gaze,
they formed a magic conjuring ring,
opening a passage to Tír na nÓg;

I hear them beckoning me still,
eager to share that island paradise,
far from the shadow of the Mourne Mountains.

citadel at the end of all things

beneath the apathetic infinitude –
the somnolent, boundless, black abyss
stretched beyond vision and reason
by the intractable influence of dark energy –
a handful of stubborn survivors persist,
too stubborn to surrender to their fixed fate.

frozen worlds wander far afield,
abandoning dead suns in starless heavens –
the monoliths of galactic empires fade
as the names of civilizations forged
fall victim to cosmic indifference
and the inevitability of oblivion.

tucked away in a humble bastion –
the citadel at the end of all things –
living meager lives on borrowed time,
dependent upon ancient technology
they neither understand nor appreciate,
they cling to existence on the edge of extinction.

Wearing Winter Gray
By Lee Clark Zumpe

Atmospheric poetry at its finest is found in Wearing Winter Gray. Lee Clark Zumpe sets his moods and draws forth evocative images and memories, and not a little emotion. Now and then a ray of light shines through his words, so that having created a somber mood, he punctuates it with a bit of joy. Thus it is that Wearing Winter Gray reminds us that Shiny Summer Colors are just around the corner.

Ordering links:

Print: https://www.hiraethsffh.com/product-page/wearing-winter-gray-by-lee-clark-zumpe

ePub: https://www.hiraethsffh.com/product-page/wearing-winter-gray-by-lee-clark-zumpe-2

PDF: https://www.hiraethsffh.com/product-page/wearing-winter-gray-by-lee-clark-zumpe-1

Corvus corax

I set out to ascertain what more might be said of you –
beyond that which is held over from Old World
superstition or inferred from those legendary lines of
lamentation scrawled once upon a midnight drab and
dismal.

Harbinger of winter, conductor of lost souls,
sable passerine of sturdy wing, firm fortitude, and
shrill cry –

your opportunistic scavenging, feasting on carrion,
too often posts you in somber graveyards or bloody
battlefields.

Huginn and Muninn, at Odin's behest, soar daily over
Midgard; I'm told one raven ferried the devil's contract
for Faust to sign, while another brought bread to a
hungry prophet; One earned the wrath of Noah;
another, praise from Norse warriors.

Discounting your intermittently ghoulish appetite,
and the imposition of imprecise allegorical qualities,
one wonders if your uncanny indicators of intellect
and capacity for abstract thought signals some
sinister agenda.

lunar landscapes

who has walked upon the surface of the moon –
experienced its unique physiography,
kicked up clouds of powdery dust
and disturbed the lunar regolith?

who has conferred with Khonsu,
the hawk-headed god of the moon,
while eating dates sweetened with honey
and admiring dancers with eyes outlined with kohl?

who has comforted Mētztli
when his fear of the sun's fire flusters him,
soothing him with reassurances
and the promise of night's benevolent stars?

who has accompanied Selene
on her nightly flight across the heavens,
driving her silver moon chariot,
eager to be reunited with sleeping Endymion?

who has dreamed of visiting lunar landscapes,
of making a pilgrimage to Tranquility Base
where footprints left by Armstrong and Aldrin
attest to the ingenuity of humanity.

Whispers from the Intoxicating Abyss
By Lee Clark Zumpe

You may not realize it, but they're out there: impossible shadows, omniscient horrors, and unseen, unknowable entities scattered across the great gulfs of nothingness at the edges of the universe. In this collection, author Lee Clark Zumpe draws back the curtain from the invisible realm, divulging its arcane secrets and ghastly revelations. Come walk paths meandering over shunned worlds adrift in darkness, and through seemingly mundane, liminal spaces that might be overrun with ancient shadows at any moment.

Stories are inspired by the works of H. P. Lovecraft.

Ordering links:
Print: https://www.hiraethsffh.com/product-page/whispers-from-the-intoxicating-abyss-by-lee-clark-zumpe

ePub: https://www.hiraethsffh.com/product-page/whispers-from-the-intoxicating-abyss-by-lee-clark-zumpe-2

PDF: https://www.hiraethsffh.com/product-page/whispers-from-the-intoxicating-abyss-by-lee-clark-zumpe-1

through the lych-gate

down a wandering, cobbled lane
lined with dilapidated cottages,
crumbling walls and vacant archways –
I seek their disembodied voices.

down to the pathway through the wood,
beyond the lines of tangled hedgerows
and long-neglected orchards –
I follow their insistent whispers.

down through the lych-gate,
where ancient yew-trees congregate
serving as silent sentries –
I obey their adamant appeals.

down to shadow-haunted ruins,
the sacred stones of a medieval church,
and its tenebrous basement bonehouse –
I fall prey to their voracious despair.

Belladonna by Sandy DeLuca

Minimalism:
A Handbook of Minimalist Genre Poetic Forms

This handbook contains articles about how to write various minimalist poetry forms such as scifaiku, senryu, sijo, haibun, empat perkataan, ghazals, cinquain, cherita, rengays, rengu, octains, tanka, threesomes, and many more. Each article is written by an expert in that particular poetry form.

Teri Santitoro, aka sakyu, who assembled this handbook, has been the editor of Scifaikuest since 2003.

https://www.hiraethsffh.com/product-page/minimalism-a-handbook-of-minimalist-genre-poetic-forms

Forbidden Haibun: K2-18B
Francis W. Alexander

Cassiopeia –
our ship slowly pierces
the planet's outer skin.

Spring dawn – this huge rock holds nothing but water and clouds. Calm green sea - our bathyscaphe inches downward. Port window – the sense of being a fossil encased in emerald.

Draco –
the only sign of life
gravity's gnashing maw

First blossoms – as the sub starts its climb sandcastles are discovered. Jolt – an angelfish-kraken pushing the bathyscaphe upwards. Scarlett sky – moments before the hurricane hits, our ship lifts off.

K2-18B -
the continent-sized tsunami
clears our spot

The Guy Belleranti Triad

scary sky tonight
no moon or starlight
just those eyes watching

alien aircraft
becomes beautiful bird
shapeshifter spaceship

two scarecrows in love
could be a dangerous match
one of them smokes

Stars sink like sand grains
In the globe of an hourglass
Time slipping away

K. S. Hardy

Cinderella's Coachmen
K. S. Hardy

For one night
We walked upright
For one night
We wore clothes
Silk stockings
Coats and breeches
Of gold satin,
Lace at our collars
Feathers in our caps.
For one night
We were supporting players
In a bigger play.
For one night
We were without tails
For one night
We were the tale
Albeit a small part
But every time it is told
Our honor is assured.

They Rattle Past in the Dark
Holly Day

This city is not real. I scuttle to safety like a roach, like a shadow to the cage I call home, down the stairs, into the dark, beneath the streets pocked by hard shoes and pointed heels, beneath the zombie metronome feet of slaves to prosperity, soldiers of fortune that drum beyond my sky at night. I can pretend the sound of them walking is something else, more trains, horses, monsters.

The others down here are strange and dark and quiet are weird. They eat each other. I've heard they eat each other. They're not my friends because I don't want to be eaten.

No one knows I'm here, not my mother, not my father, not my last place of employment, here, in this little hole in the wall of the tunnel, a cave of crumbling brick and twisted rebar metal wheel lightning my own source of sunshine, bright enough to read by but too intermittent to read by. Sometimes I can see the faces of the passengers through the windows of the cars, I can see them looking out the windows, too out into the dark, eyes bright and scared, they can't see me.

The Beauty of a Changeling
Kellee Kranendonk

Shifting, moving
  Always different
    One day shimmering rain
      The next a galloping horse
        Wind soaring through your mane
          Gliding, fluid movement
            Ever changing, gradient like
              The colours of a sunset
          Smooth, flowing
        Perpetually capricious
      One day a rainbow
     The next bioluminescence
   As if change is easy
    Requiring no effort
     No thought
       Just the sublime transformation
        Of living, breathing energy

Featured Poet: Allister Nelson

Golden Cow, Silver Milk

Babushka lives down the stairs,
don't you know?

Clean, spin, sew.

Milk golden cows for silver milk,
she has chores to do, a bone fence,
leshys to play chess with and a mortar
and pestle to beat black and blue her
suitors with.

If you come courting
Baba Yaga, best bring some blood
and wine. Chicken bones. A skull
lantern.

Meet with her and beat
your breasts under a new moon in
ancient rites of witchcraft, and she
is my mother, my ancestress, the
hag of the forest I call my kin,
wise woman and baby eater,
like Lilith but wilder and not
a beauty, like Angrboda with none
of the red tangling hair, just
a kerchief and shock white braid.
She is churning out your future
into butter for blini, eat some
of her pierogis and listen to me,

knitting and woman's work is
sacred, and be you a good little
girl, dutiful daughter and diligent,
she shall take you to her side and
teach you all sorts of arcane magic.

I have Baba Yaga in my basement,
quite literally, and I always make
sure to pour her the finest of drinks.

Pumpkin Spice

Lady October is bird-like
with a quirk of her head to the side
quick with a laugh and lighter
she chain smokes like James Dean
(only Chesterfields, I'm told)
and chuckles like clinking keys

I met her once at a bar in Cleveland
she was out on the steps in the gloaming
taking shots of rain
in a little black dress
that glossed over
her skin like a siren's tongue

I asked her for her number, smitten
she gave me a string of autumn leaves:

"Roll and smoke these, you'll find me
but be warned, I never leave."

She smiled like the evening
and flew away on a harvest breeze

I smoked them, every frond
and in the blue-black plumes
followed her home

She nests in a swallow-tail apartment
the floors downy with dreams

We made love (or did we?) after wine
she tasted of country apples, so ripe
I felt starved for days

October never leaves you
once marked, her cigarette butts
brand your soul

Ashes of her will
linger -

In little corners of your house.

Your mind will stray to her
In the small hours

October, October, come home

Her voice is a sage's whisper
a quiet becoming in a lover's breast.

She is the color of rose-gold and
the first blush of a virgin's awakening.

Her clavicle is tattooed with a key
that opens doors to Father Time's throne.

She took me there and we wandered
through golden halls studded with trees

When October mourns, she goes there
to a grove hidden behind the stars.

It has the graves of her sister months
whom she rarely sees, these days

We toasted November's mausoleum
and put daisies on July

I let my arm linger at the
base of October's waist.
I made promises I'll never keep

She smiled and plucked
a forget-me-not

It was the 31st.

Next morning, I buried her
(in snow, or was it old newspaper?)

I made a fort of the stuff

Sometimes, I think of her dreaming
waiting for a spring
she'll never
see.

Defect
Debby Feo

My tail kept slipping out
My claws tore my fake hands
More false assurances

Lots of money changed hands
Binding garments squished me
Deodorants failed me

A tickle in my throat
Also threatened disguise
Drank to hold down my fire

Needed nine more minutes
To reach my assigned suite
Escape from home planet

Unwanted dragon-man
Plagued with wanderlust
And extraneous parts

I was not successful
Yet again captured
Must proceed to plan D

Not Cupid's Arrows
Shawn Vimislicky

He had ducked, dived and jumped,
   all to successfully avoid the many
  of Cupid's golden and leaden tipped arrows.
Then one night stepping out into the moonlight,
   there came a Muse unnamed by Zeus
   and unacknowledged by her nine sisters.
A Muse confused about her capabilities for inspiring
any artistry, she disappeared into speculative spaces
filled with otherworldly faces.
It was she who shot with accuracy
  the arrow that sunk and stuck in his dreamy mind.
Love struck he became, love struck for every subject
or object the arrow tip had previously touched or
pricked.

Now he receives daily or nightly
  dreamy visions involving all or many of his loves.
His love for a blue moon goddess and a star dust
princess, for changelings, endlings, flying lizards, and
bone wizards,
  for knights and damsels in castles made of crystals.
His love for red headed wild hearted witches,
  their azure eyes aglow and veinless skin
  as white as snow.
His love for mixing griffon blood with dragon blood,
  the two thickened with grated green gorgon skull,
  and all, added to a honey based alcohol.

Some loves he holds tight under blue moonlight,
  from some he'll run in moments of laughter and fun,
  others keep him wary for their moods and passions
  he finds scary,
     but all are exciting and inspiring.
These loves sustaining him daily and nightly,
  leaving him barely needing any
  subjects or objects from waking reality.
While a Muse unnamed
   moves steadily from dreamy heights and depths,
   from moonlight to darkened corners making new arrows,
   arrows never to be tipped golden or leaden.

A Goldilocks Alien Exploration of the Solar System

Francis W. Alexander

the second planet from its sun
is too hot
the fourth planet from the sun
is too cold

Goldilocks loved the look
of the third planet.

Disappointed,
because it stank of death
and was too irradiated.

Nuit's Garden
Anthony Bernstein

Peel away the skin from the sky
to discover her wild ballet
across the sweeping stellar winds.
View her kaleidoscopic visage
traced upon creations' fluid horizon.
Glimpse her likeness as she springs
from the splitting atom.

She sings the spindrift of nebulas
plays midwife to a nursery of newborn stars.
She looms the mystery-fabric of time-space,
sows her seeds across the fertile fields of eternity—
every seed, a new world, a new chance
for deadly magnificence, poisonous beauty, life.

If you could breach the depths of a black hole
you would find her within dancing
the mysteries and courting the chaos
With elegance and Starpower.
As one who loves so absolutely,
she weaves the nimbus web of creation
from her ever-flowing stream of starlight hair.

She walks galaxies in easy strides,
for she engineers the boundless dark
that accelerates them to oblivion.

The Heart of the Song
Holly Day

Make your cuts, carefully relieve the tendons
Of their nested burden, pull it out, fist-sized, raw
Drop it in the mason jar filled with cognac, seal it
tight.

If there are memories stored in cells, perhaps one day
Someone will lift my heart from this jar
Find the songs left still unwritten

Half-hummed compositions laid to rest
Symphonies yet to be realized.

Lifeboats
Amanda Niamh Dawson

Coming fast
Life's deep edge
Wheel of light

Great unbound
Wound around
Circle's ending
Stars are sending
Flights upending
Floating suspended
Waiting
'Til time
World has ended

The Old Fisherman
Joy Yin

Every full moon
Ripples glide through the clear water
Old fisherman's boat creeks through.

His eyes are old
Bitten by the frosts of time
Staring at the moon

There sprouts a silver trail
Between boat and pearly marble
The old fisherman follows it
Up.

Sailing on the moon
He reunites with his lover
Long lost to the cruel stars.
As he releases
His space helmet.

www.ingramcontent.com/pod-product-compliance
Lightning Source LLC
LaVergne TN
LVHW092100060526
838201LV00047B/1491